Pancakes!

Written by Judy Nayer
Illustrated by Judith Stuller Hannant

Pat-a-cake, pat-a-cake, baker's man.
Make some pancakes as fast as
you can!

Pancakes for breakfast,
pancakes for a snack,

I love pancakes.
Give me a stack.

Mix the batter.
Pour it in the pan.

Make some pancakes
as fast as you can.

Big ones, little ones,
make a big batch.

Flip them, flap them,
get ready to catch.

Pat-a-cake, pat-a-cake, baker's man.
Make some pancakes as fast as
you can.

Pancakes on the table,
pancakes on the plate,

12

pancakes everywhere—
I can't wait.

Pancakes on the ceiling,
pancakes on the floor,

I love pancakes . . .

Let's make some more!